Montana
Wildlife

A beginner's field guide
to the state's most
remarkable animals

Interpreting the Great Outdoors
Text by Gayle C. Shirley, Illustrations by Sandy Allnock

For my parents, Marshall and Jean Corbett, with love.
Thanks for nudging me in all the right directions.—GCS

For Gay, with thanks for the encouragement
and valued teachings.—SA

FALCON™

© 1993 by Falcon Press Publishing Co., Inc.,
Billings and Helena, Montana.

On the front cover: Grizzly bear, bald eagle, pronghorn, cutthroat trout, and western rattlesnake.

Design, editing, typesetting, and other prepress work by Falcon Press, Helena, Montana. Printed in Malaysia.

Library of Congress Number 92-055081
ISBN 1-56044-154-2

Contents

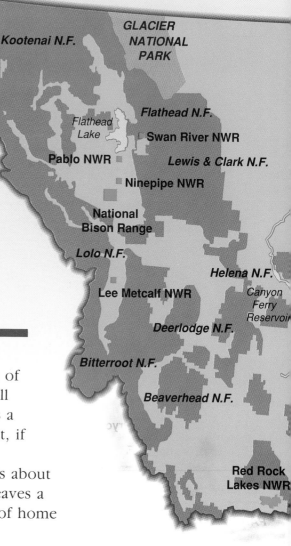

Kootenai N.F.

GLACIER
NATIONAL
PARK

Flathead
Lake

Flathead N.F.

Swan River NWR

Pablo NWR

Lewis & Clark N.F.

Ninepipe NWR

National
Bison Range

Lolo N.F.

Helena N.F.

Lee Metcalf NWR

Canyon
Ferry
Reservoir

Deerlodge N.F.

Bitterroot N.F.

Beaverhead N.F.

Red Rock
Lakes NWR

Introduction

Montana is a paradise for many kinds of wildlife. The land, air, and water are still fairly clean and natural. And Montana is a big state with a small population. In fact, if you can imagine the state cut up into chunks the size of football fields, there's about one person for every 106 fields. That leaves a lot of wide open spaces—just the kind of home most wild animals like best.

There are 357 different kinds of birds, 108 mammals, 86 fish, 17 reptiles, and 16 amphibians in Montana. As you page through this book, you'll see that they're big and small, cute and ugly, fuzzy and slimy, fierce and shy. Every animal is unique. Each occupies its own special habitat and has its own strategy for survival. And each has a place in the web of life.

One reason Montana wildlife is so varied is that the landscape is varied, too. You'll find everything from mountains, foothills, and prairies to deserts, forests, and wetlands. In the west, the jagged Rockies take a mighty bite out of the Big Sky. Clean, cold streams and rivers tumble through the valleys. Forests blanket the lower slopes, while wind slaps the rocky peaks above. Bears, bighorn sheep, and bald eagles are just a few of the creatures that make the western mountains their home.

In the east, Montana is mostly rolling prairie, a huge expanse of golden grasses beaten by wind, rain, snow, and hail and dotted with islands of

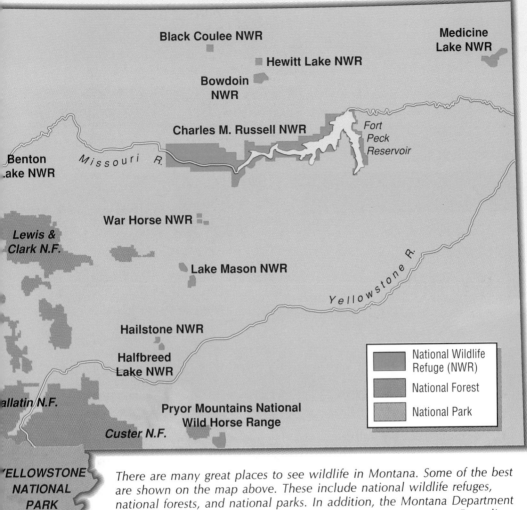

Black Coulee NWR

Medicine Lake NWR

Hewitt Lake NWR

Bowdoin NWR

Charles M. Russell NWR

Fort Peck Reservoir

Benton Lake NWR

Missouri R.

War Horse NWR

Lewis & Clark N.F.

Lake Mason NWR

Yellowstone R.

Hailstone NWR

Halfbreed Lake NWR

Gallatin N.F.

Pryor Mountains National Wild Horse Range

Custer N.F.

YELLOWSTONE NATIONAL PARK

	National Wildlife Refuge (NWR)
	National Forest
	National Park

There are many great places to see wildlife in Montana. Some of the best are shown on the map above. These include national wildlife refuges, national forests, and national parks. In addition, the Montana Department of Fish, Wildlife and Parks has 62 Wildlife Management Areas. For a list of these areas, please contact the department headquarters in Helena, phone (406) 444-2535. Many areas also are described in the Montana Wildlife Viewing Guide. *(See page 47)*

hills and trees. Temperatures can be extreme. The summer sun can bake the land, while the winter cold can lock it in ice. The animals that live here are hardy creatures. Over the centuries, they've adapted to their prairie home. Coyotes, pronghorns, and rattlesnakes are among those that have learned to survive, and even thrive, in eastern Montana.

Montana has some of the best wildlife habitat in the country. So it's not surprising that this is one of the best states in which to see wild animals. They're watching you as you hike through the forests, drive across the plains, or sit beside a mountain lake. They may even be watching you from your own backyard. Why not take the time to stop and watch them, too? They'll always amaze you.

Prairies

When most people think of Montana, they think of mountains. But two-thirds of the state is rolling prairie. Life can be harsh on the plains. In the summer, the sun can scorch the prairie grasses. In the winter, high winds and bitter cold can lock the land in ice.

At first glance, the prairie looks barren and lifeless. But the animals that live here have adapted well to extreme conditions. Some escape the heat and cold in burrows, like the prairie dog and badger. Others grow thick coats for protection, like the coyote, pronghorn, and bison. Most seek shelter when the weather is at its worst.

The prairie is full of life, if only we are patient enough to find it.

Pronghorn

other names: antelope, pronghorn antelope
habitat: grasslands, sagebrush plains
food: grasses and shrubs, mostly sagebrush
size: 75-140 pounds, up to 3.5 feet tall at shoulder
reproduction: usually twins born May-June
status: common east of Rocky Mountains
scientific name: *Antilocapra americana*

The pronghorn is the fastest land animal in North America. It can run 40-50 miles an hour—almost as fast as a car travels on the highway. It has even been known to reach 84 miles an hour for short distances!

According to an old Blackfeet Indian legend, the Blackfeet creator "Old Man" made the pronghorn out of dirt while he was in the mountains. But when he set his creature free, it ran so fast it tripped over the rocks. So Old Man took it to the prairie. There, the pronghorn could run swiftly and gracefully, and Old Man was pleased.

Bison

other names: buffalo
habitat: grasslands, open woodlands
food: grasses, leaves, shrubs, twigs
size: 800-2,000 pounds, 5-6 feet tall at hump, largest land animal in North America
reproduction: 1 calf born April-May
status: exists mostly in managed herds
scientific name: *Bison bison*

More than 30 million bison once blackened the plains of North America. Some herds were so big they took a week to pass by.

Plains Indians took advantage of the bison's strong herd instinct. Sometimes they would spook a herd into stampeding and then drive it toward a high cliff known as a *pishkun*, or buffalo jump. By the time the lead animals knew where they were headed, it was too late to stop. They plunged over the cliff, and the rest of the herd followed.

Coyote

other names: prairie wolf
habitat: prefers prairies but will live anywhere
food: eats almost anything, plant or animal
size: 30-40 pounds, 43-53 inches long
reproduction: 4-7 pups born March-May
status: common statewide, important fur animal
scientific name: *Canis latrans*

If the prairie has a voice, it's the haunting howl of the coyote. The concert usually begins at dusk or dawn. One animal points its nose at the stars and utters a long, mournful wail followed by a series of yips and yaps. Other coyotes within hearing distance join in. They sing with so much gusto that three or four animals can sound like a dozen.

Coyotes use their howls to "talk" to their mates or pups over long distances—to warn of danger, tell of food, or ask for help. But they also seem to sing just for the fun of it. To many people, their song has become a symbol of the wide open spaces.

Badger

other names: none
habitat: dry, open country
food: ground squirrels, other small mammals, birds, eggs, reptiles
size: 13-25 pounds, 22-28 inches long
reproduction: 1-4 cubs born March-April
status: common statewide
scientific name: *Taxidea taxus*

The badger is a powerful digging machine. It digs for food and to make a place to sleep. First it loosens the dirt with its 1- to 2-inch claws. Then it flings the dirt aside with toes that are partly webbed. It can burrow out of sight in only a few minutes, creating a little dirt blizzard as it goes.

Because it's short and squat and has very loose skin, the badger looks almost comical. But it has a quick temper and will snarl, growl, and hiss when threatened. It's a savage fighter. Few predators dare to tangle with it.

Black-footed ferret

other names: none
habitat: prairies
food: mostly prairie dogs
size: 20-24 inches long
reproduction: 3-5 young born late spring or early
    summer
status: endangered species
scientific name: *Mustela nigripes*

This member of the weasel family may be the rarest mammal on earth. In 1987, only 18 were known to exist in the wild. They were all captured by the Wyoming Game and Fish Department, which is breeding them in captivity to keep the animal from becoming extinct. So far, the breeding program has been successful, and a few animals have been set free in Wyoming.

In Montana, only 39 black-footed ferrets have been seen for sure. The last was spotted on a ranch near Ekalaka in 1977. Some of the Wyoming ferrets may be set free in Phillips County, in northeastern Montana. Wildlife officials hope to release them in the fall of 1993.

Black-tailed prairie dog

other names: none
habitat: short-grass prairies
food: grasses and other green plants
size: 2-3 pounds, 12-16 inches long
reproduction: 3-8 pups born April-May
status: common east of Continental Divide
scientific name: *Cynomys ludovicianus*

Close to five billion prairie dogs once lived in huge, connected "towns" across the Great Plains. But the prairie dogs ate the grass the settlers wanted for their cattle. So settlers tried to get rid of them, killing them by the thousands.

Today, prairies dogs live in relatively small, scattered colonies. One of the easiest to visit is the Greycliff Prairie Dog Town, about seven miles east of Big Timber on Interstate 90. There, you can watch these busy little creatures dig and repair their maze of underground tunnels. They live in one of the most elaborate homes made by any American mammal.

Red-tailed hawk

other names: redtail, buzzard, chicken hawk
habitat: prairies, open woodlands, farm country
food: mostly rodents
size: 2.5-3.5 pounds, 19-25 inches long, wingspan
    about 4 feet
reproduction: 2-3 white eggs with brown
    spots, laid in April
status: common statewide
scientific name: *Buteo jamaicensis*

The red-tailed hawk is one of 16 kinds of hawks in Montana. It's also one of the largest and best-known. The redtail has excellent eyesight. It can spot a tiny mouse from high in the sky. When it does, it dives at 120 miles an hour, nabbing its dinner before the unlucky main course can even utter a squeak.

The redtail isn't terribly picky about what it eats. It will even dine on rattlesnakes and skunks—despite their unpleasant ways of defending themselves.

White-tailed jackrabbit

other names: snowshoe rabbit
habitat: open country from plains to mountain
    slopes
food: green plants in summer, shrubs in winter
size: 5-8 pounds, 18-22 inches long
reproduction: 3-8 young born May-October
status: common in all but extreme northwestern
    Montana
scientific name: *Lepus townsendii*

The jackrabbit doesn't have ears half a foot long for nothing! Its hearing is so keen it can detect the faint swish of a coyote's fur brushing against the prairie grasses.

When a predator such as the coyote approaches, the jackrabbit may freeze in place, counting on its grayish-brown coloring to help it blend into its surroundings. In winter, its fur turns white so it can hide in the snow. If camouflage doesn't work, it will dash away at up to 35 miles an hour. With powerful hind legs, it can easily clear more than 10 feet in a single leap.

Sage grouse

other names: sage chicken
habitat: sagebrush plains
food: sagebrush, green plants, insects
size: 2.5-7 pounds, 21-30 inches long
reproduction: 7-8 pale green eggs with brown dots,
    laid March-June
status: native to Montana, common game bird in
    eastern and southwestern parts of state
scientific name: *Centrocercus urophasianus*

The things a male sage grouse has to go through to get a girl! In March, as breeding season nears, the males gather on traditional dancing grounds to strut their stuff and impress the females. They shuffle their feet, spread their tail feathers, and let their wings droop. With a jerking motion of the head, each male puffs up a pair of balloon-like sacs on its breast. Then it lets the air out with a loud popping noise.

Female sage grouse find the whole show very attractive. They flock to the dancing grounds to mate.

Prairie falcon

other names: none
habitat: cliffs for nesting, prairies for hunting
food: birds, small mammals
size: about 2 pounds, 17-20 inches long, wingspan
    3.5 feet
reproduction: 4-5 white eggs marked with brown,
    purple; usually laid in late April
status: species of special concern in
    Montana, more common east of
    Continental Divide
scientific name: *Falco mexicanus*

The prairie falcon cruises at 30 miles an hour—almost as fast as its darker cousin, the peregrine falcon. It can overtake most other birds in flight. When hunting, it can knock a smaller bird from the sky with its feet or grab it in midair. But it takes most of its prey by descending in a long, slanting swoop and plucking it from the ground.

The prairie falcon is a short-tempered bird. It will pester larger and slower hawks and eagles if they come near its nest. You're most likely to see prairie falcons in and near the canyons and cliffs where they like to make their nests. These are usually just scrapes in the dirt or gravel.

Western meadowlark

other names: none
habitat: prairies, meadows, pastures
food: insects, seeds
size: about 3 ounces, 8-11 inches long
reproduction: usually 5 white eggs with brown
     spots, sometimes two batches a year
status: official state bird, common statewide
scientific name: *Sturnella neglecta*

Few sounds announce spring as clearly as the bubbling melody of the meadowlark. Its song is useful as well as beautiful. With it, the male attracts potential mates and warns rivals to stay out of its territory.

The female lays her eggs in a well-hidden nest on the ground. To keep enemies from finding it, she hardly ever flies directly to it. She lands 20-50 feet away and then walks the rest of the way. When she leaves the nest, she also walks away before she flies off.

Western rattlesnake

other names: prairie rattler
habitat: rocky parts of prairies
food: small mammals, birds, lizards
size: 15-62 inches long
reproduction: born live, about 12 in a brood
status: poisonous, common in eastern Montana
scientific name: *Crotalus viridis*

Watch out for this poisonous reptile! If you disturb it, it may try to warn you away with a loud buzzing noise. It makes the sound by shaking the rattles at the tip of its tail. Given the chance, it would rather flee than bite you. Still, the rattlesnake is among the four most poisonous snakes in the United States. Its bite is painful. Although it doesn't always kill, it can cause infection and serious illness.

To avoid meeting a rattlesnake unexpectedly, be careful around prairie-dog towns, rocky areas, and sagebrush thickets along prairie roads—especially in the mornings and evenings.

11

Mountain Forests & Meadows

Compared to the prairies, mountain forests and meadows are a green and inviting place to live. Water and hiding places are plentiful, and temperatures don't stray far from the middle of the thermometer.

Here, you'll see colorful birds flitting among the trees. A squirrel scolding a black bear scratching its back against a tree trunk. Mule deer grazing in the meadows, their long ears swiveling to catch the stealthy approach of a mountain lion.

For many species, the pine, fir, birch, and aspen trees that blanket the western third of the state provide food as well as shelter from predators and the weather. So when you hike through the mountains, keep your eyes and ears open. You're not alone.

Elk

other names: wapiti
habitat: coniferous forests dotted by meadows
food: grasses, leaves, twigs
size: 500-1,000 pounds, 4-5 feet tall at shoulder
reproduction: 1 calf born May-June
status: popular game animal well-established in western Montana and a few parts of eastern Montana
scientific name: *Cervus elaphus*

In the fall, one of the most exciting sounds you can hear in the forest is the bugle of bull elk as they challenge each other for the right to mate with the females, or cows. Usually the bull with the most threatening bugle also has the largest antlers. He will be king of the herd. Just a glimpse of his impressive "rack" may be enough to discourage the competition.

After the mating season, bull elk shed their antlers. Then, in the spring, they begin to grow new, larger ones. The antlers of a full-grown bull elk can reach 4-5 feet long. The distance between the tips of the antlers can reach 5 feet. That's as wide as the elk is tall!

Mule deer

other names: black-tailed deer
habitat: grasslands, brushy areas, mountain forests and meadows
food: twigs, grasses, moss, leaves
size: 160-275 pounds, 3-3.5 feet tall at shoulder
reproduction: 1-2 spotted fawns born in June
status: game animal, common statewide
scientific name: *Odocoileus hemionus*

When a mule deer perks its ears to listen for danger, it's easy to see how it got its name. Its ears are bigger than those of the white-tailed deer, which is also common in the forests and along tree-lined rivers and streams throughout Montana. There are other ways to tell the two kinds of deer apart. The mule deer is the one with black on its tail. And unlike the whitetail, it keeps its tail down as it bounds away through the underbrush.

Grizzly bear

other names: silvertip, brown bear
habitat: wilderness forests and meadows
food: grasses, roots, bulbs, berries, insects, meat
size: 200-550 pounds, 6-7 feet long
reproduction: usually 2 cubs born in winter den
    every 3-5 years
status: official state animal, threatened species
scientific name: *Ursus arctos horribilis*

Thousands of grizzlies once roamed the West. Explorers, trappers, and settlers all had horrible stories about the great bear. But as civilization came west, people did all they could to destroy the grizzly. As they built homes and planted crops, they robbed it of its habitat.

Today, only about 600-800 grizzlies live in Montana. Most are along the Continental Divide between Glacier and Yellowstone national parks. Still, Montana has the biggest grizzly population south of Canada. The bear has become a symbol of the wilderness because it needs wild, undeveloped country to survive.

Grizzlies are often described as ferocious meat-eaters—even man-eaters. But in fact, as much as 90 percent of their diet is made up of plants. And most do their best to avoid people, their only enemy.

Black bear

other names: American black bear, cinnamon bear
habitat: dense forests, near water
food: grasses, berries, fruits, tree bark, insects,
    honey, eggs, dead animals, rodents, occasional
    hooved animals
size: 100-400 pounds, 5-6 feet long
reproduction: similar to grizzlies
status: good numbers in mountains of western and
    southcentral Montana
scientific name: *Ursus americanus*

How would you like to have to go 5-7 months without eating, drinking, or using the bathroom? Sound impossible? Bears do it every winter, when they're asleep in their dens. And they wake up just as healthy as they were in the fall.

Bears don't sleep through the winter to avoid the cold. They do it to get through the months when there's not much to eat. Curled in their dens, they survive on the fat they stored by overeating in the fall.

Bears hibernate differently from some other animals. The marmot, for example, has to wake up every few days to eat, drink, and relieve itself. When it *is* asleep, nothing can rouse it. Bears will wake up if they're disturbed. In fact, female bears give birth in the winter den. They wake up whenever their cubs cry for attention.

Gray wolf

other names: timber wolf
habitat: wilderness forests, tundra
food: deer, elk, moose, bighorn sheep, small
     mammals, berries, fruits
size: 70-170 pounds, 26-28 inches tall at shoulder
reproduction: 4-6 pups born March-April
status: endangered species
scientific name: *Canis lupus*

Wolves are close relatives of the dog, and like man's best friend they can be very loyal. When a young female chooses her mate, they usually stay partners for life. If one dies, the other may never mate again.

The day before giving birth, a pregnant female usually crawls away from the pack. Her mate stands guard while she has her pups. Right after the young are born, the mother leaves them only to get a drink. Her mate brings her food.

When the pups are old enough to leave their den—at about three weeks—the other members of the wolf pack are excited to see them. They even take turns "babysitting" while the mother goes off to hunt.

Mountain lion

other names: cougar, puma, panther, catamount
habitat: mostly mountains and foothills
food: mostly deer, elk, and porcupines
size: 70-190 pounds, 6-8 feet long including tail
reproduction: 1-5 kittens born May-July every 2-3
     years
status: common game animal in mountains and
     foothills, occasional in eastern Montana
scientific name: *Felis concolor*

The mountain lion is an awesome predator. Unlike other wild cats, it will attack animals bigger than it is—even five times bigger! It's not uncommon for an adult mountain lion to take down a 500-pound bull elk. It's also one of the few predators that will tangle with the prickly porcupine. It just flips the animal over with its paws and bites into its soft belly.

Like a phantom in the forest, the mountain lion stalks its prey silently, on soft, padded feet. It's most active at night, and it usually tries to avoid humans. Few people ever see one in the wild.

Bobcat and Lynx

other names: wildcat
habitat: bobcat prefers rocky areas with trees or shrubs for cover; lynx likes forests at higher elevations
food: mostly snowshoe hares, cottontail rabbits, jackrabbits
size: 15-35 pounds, 28-37 inches long
reproduction: 2-4 kittens born April-May
status: bobcat common statewide, lynx occasional in western Montana, both valuable fur animals
scientific name: bobcat *Felis rufus*, lynx *Felis lynx*

These two wildcats may look and act a lot alike, but they're hardly kissing cousins. In places where both can be found, they try hard to avoid each other. Like the mountain lion, they're shy and solitary animals.

The lynx may grow a little larger than the bobcat. It also has longer tufts of fur at the tips of its ears, longer legs, and larger paws. Its paws are very furry and act like snowshoes, helping the cat to move over the deep, soft snows of its high mountain home. Bobcats just move to lower elevations in the winter, where there's less snow to deal with.

*Lynx
(bobcat not shown)*

Snowshoe hare

other names: varying hare, snowshoe rabbit
habitat: swampy areas, coniferous forests, brushy areas
food: grasses and other plants in summer, tree bark and buds in winter
size: 2-4 pounds, 13-18 inches long
reproduction: 3-8 young born two or more times a year
status: periodically common in northwestern Montana
scientific name: *Lepus americanus*

The snowshoe hare is the main food of the lynx, so their lives are closely connected. When there are lots of snowshoe hares, there are soon more lynx. When the hare population shrinks because there's not enough food, the lynx population drops, too. About every 8-11 years, the two animals go through this cycle of population growth and decline.

One way the snowshoe hare tries to escape the lynx and other predators is by turning from a mottled brown in the summer to white in the winter. The color change helps the animal blend into its surroundings year-round.

Porcupine

other names: hedgehog
habitat: forests
food: twigs, leaves, buds in summer; inner bark of
    trees, pine needles in winter
size: 10-30 pounds, 25-31 inches long with tail
reproduction: 1 porcupette born in spring
status: common in western Montana
scientific name: *Erethizon dorsatum*

Because of its 30,000 sharp quills, the porcupine doesn't have to worry much about enemies. If an animal or person is foolish enough to come close, the porcupine gnashes its teeth and rattles its quills. It can't throw the quills like spears, as some people used to believe. But it can swing its tail like a spiked club. The tip of each quill is covered with barbs like the ones on a fishhook. This makes them hard to pull out.

Porcupines are born with a full set of quills. At first they're soft, but within hours they're as sharp and hard as those of an adult. When quills come out, the animal just grows new ones.

Red squirrel

other names: chickaree, boomer, pine squirrel
habitat: coniferous forests
food: mostly nuts, berries, fruits, seeds
size: 5-11 ounces, 11-14 inches long with tail
reproduction: 1-7 young in litter, 1-2 litters a year
status: abundant in western Montana forests
scientific name: *Tamiasciurus hudsonicus*

You may never see it, but you'll know it's there. The red squirrel is the chatterbox of the forest—saucy and loud. From a safe perch high in a tree, it chatters, barks, and scolds. It lets you know in no uncertain terms that you're trespassing on its territory.

The red squirrel is sometimes known as the sentinel of the forest. It notices everything and reacts noisily to anything out of the ordinary. Many other animals heed the little squirrel's alarm.

Northern flicker

other names: red-shafted flicker, red-hammer
habitat: woodlands, deserts, suburbs
food: mostly insects
size: about 4.5 ounces, 12-14 inches long
reproduction: 5-8 white eggs laid May-June
status: common statewide in summer, uncommon
    in winter
scientific name: *Colaptes auratus*

Next time you go on a picnic, you might want to invite a flicker along. While you nibble on a chicken drumstick, it will keep the ants away—by eating them!

Ants are the flicker's favorite food. In fact, it eats more of them than any other bird in North America. That's why the flicker spends so much time on the ground, even though it's a member of the woodpecker family. Like an anteater, the flicker laps up the ants with its tongue, which is almost 3 inches longer than its beak.

Gray jay

other names: camp robber, Canada jay, whiskey
    jack
habitat: coniferous forests
food: insects, fruit, seeds, mice, birds' eggs, dead
    animals
size: about 2.5 ounces, 10-13 inches long,
    wingspread 16-17.5 inches
reproduction: 3-4 greenish, spotted eggs, laid
    March-April
status: common year-round in western Montana
scientific name: *Perisoreus canadensis*

You won't have to invite the gray jay on your picnic. It'll show up anyway.

The gray jay is the boldest bird in the mountains. In fact, it's a first-class mooch. It will fly right into a campground and land on a plate or frying pan to steal a bit of food. That's why it's sometimes called "camp robber." It will eat almost anything. And if you turn your back, that "anything" might be your lunch!

There's a reason the gray jay is so aggressive about finding food. It lives in the mountain forests all year—even during the winter, when food is hard to find. So it eats as much as possible while it can. And it stores food to eat later, when the snow flies. Maybe it's worth sharing your lunch with the gray jay after all.

Black-capped chickadee

other names: none
habitat: forests, gardens, towns
food: insects, seeds, berries
size: less than half an ounce, 4.5-5.5 inches long,
      wingspread 7.5-8.5 inches
reproduction: 6-8 white eggs spotted with brown,
      laid May-June
status: common statewide year-round
scientific name: *Parus atricapillus*

The black-capped chickadee is one of the most commonly seen birds in Montana. It often visits bird feeders. And in the forest, its black head stands out against the gray skies and white snows of winter.

Black-capped chickadees understand the value of cooperation. They band together in groups of 8-12 birds during the winter to improve their chances of finding food. When one finds a tidbit, the others start looking in the same area.

Calliope hummingbird

other names: hummer
habitat: mountains forests and meadows
food: flower nectar, small insects
size: .1 ounce, 2.5-3.5 inches long, wingspread
      about 4.5 inches
reproduction: usually 2 white eggs laid June-July
status: common in western Montana during summer
scientific name: *Stellula calliope*

About as long as a stick of gum, the calliope hummingbird is the smallest bird not only in Montana, but in all of North America. It's also the most amazing flier. It can move forward, backward, up, down, and sideways. And it can hover motionless in midair. It's the "helicopter" of the bird world.

When it hovers, the hummingbird's wings beat 40-60 times a second—so fast they look like a blur. During flight, they may beat as many as 200 times a second! All this motion takes a lot of energy, so hummingbirds must eat almost constantly.

Western tanager

other names: Louisiana tanager
habitat: open coniferous forests
food: insects, fruits, berries
size: 1.25 ounces, 6.5-7.5 inches long, wingspread
     11-12 inches
reproduction: 3-5 pale blue eggs spotted with
     brown, laid June-July
status: fairly common statewide in summer, but
     especially in Rockies
scientific name: *Piranga ludoviciana*

Lewis and Clark discovered the western tanager in Idaho during their famous expedition of 1804-1806. It's a native of the Rocky Mountains and may range as high as 10,000 feet.

The tanager isn't an especially good singer, but the male makes up for it by being a flashy dresser. It's one of the most colorful birds in the Rockies. The female is not as showy. Her feathers are grayish-green above and a dull yellow below.

Western bluebird

other names: California bluebird, Mexican bluebird
habitat: open coniferous forests, farms, plains and
     brush in winter
food: insects, spiders, berries
size: 1-1.25 ounces, 6-7.5 inches long
reproduction: 4-6 pale blue eggs, laid May-June
status: uncommon to rare in summer, mainly west
     of Continental Divide
scientific name: *Sialia mexicana*

The western bluebird wears the clear sky on its back and the rosy glow of dawn on its breast. As it flits through the dark branches of an evergreen forest, it's unmistakable.

This bird builds its nest above ground in a woodpecker hole or other natural cavity. As soon as one batch of eggs is hatched and the youngsters are ready to fly, the parents begin to raise a second family.

Bluebirds are popular birds. Many people put bluebird houses on fence posts to attract the colorful creatures. More than 15,000 of these houses have been put up in Montana.

Mountaintops

One step below the sky is a land shaped by wind and snow—the high country of Montana. Here, the tall forests give way to ground-hugging plants, such as grass, moss, and lichens. What few trees do survive are stunted and twisted into strange shapes by the wind. Few animals can live in this harsh world.

For most of the year, snow smothers the mountaintops, and the moaning of the wind is all that breaks the silence. Some animals head down into the trees for the winter. Those that remain have adapted to their bleak home.

Summer here is short but sweet. Dazzling wildflowers blanket the ground, fed by melting snow. The lack of trees makes it easier to see wildlife. This is the time to head to the high country.

Pika

other names: cony
habitat: high mountains, rocks
food: grasses, herbs, twigs
size: 3.5-4.5 ounces, 6-8.5 inches long
reproduction: 2-4 young born April-May
status: common in mountains
scientific name: *Ochotona princeps*

The pika is one of the few animals hardy enough to stay active in the high country all year. To survive during the winter, it spends much of the summer scampering across the rocks with its mouth full of grass and leaves. It deposits them on a growing pile, where they can dry in the sun. Before the summer's over, one tiny pika may collect as much as 30 pounds of plants. When cold weather sets in and food grows scarce, the animal simply nibbles on its summer harvest.

Hoary marmot

other names: whistler
habitat: rocky slopes near alpine meadows
food: flowering plants, berries, roots, grasses, seeds
size: 8-30 pounds, 18-21 inches long
reproduction: 2-5 young born May-June every 2-4 years
status: generally rare, common at Logan Pass in Glacier National Park
scientific name: *Marmota caligata*

Don't be surprised if you're hiking in the mountains and you hear a piercing whistle that seems to come from nowhere. It's probably just a hoary marmot hiding in the rocks. Now you know why it's called "the whistler."

The hoary marmot is the largest member of the squirrel family in Montana. Its whistle is a signal to other marmots to watch out for danger. The sound is so loud that on a calm day you can hear it a mile away.

Another good name for this rodent might be "the sleeper." During the long winters in high country, it hibernates in a den under the rocks. Its body gradually slows down until it breathes only three times a minute. Its body temperature drops, and its heart beats very slowly.

Bighorn sheep

other names: mountain sheep, Rocky Mountain
        sheep
habitat: rugged mountain slopes with few trees
food: mostly grasses
size: 150-300 pounds, 2.5-3.5 feet tall at shoulder
reproduction: usually 1 lamb born May-June
status: 27 herds in isolated mountain ranges
scientific name: *Ovis canadensis*

On a steep, rocky slope, two bighorn
rams push and shove each other. Each
wants to prove it's the most qualified to
father the herd's offspring. Eventually, the
animals turn and walk away, apparently
tired of sparring. Suddenly one spins
around, rears up on its hind legs, and
charges. His opponent does the same.
They smash their heads and horns
together with a crack that can be heard a
mile away.

Often one ram gives up and backs
away after a single charge. But some
rams have been seen clashing 48 times
in one day. Fortunately, nature provided
them with double-layered skulls and
extra-thick face skin. Like a football
helmet, these protect the animals' heads
and brains from injury.

Mountain goat

other names: Rocky Mountain goat
habitat: rocky ledges and steep slopes at or above
        timberline
food: grasses, herbs, shrubs
size: 150-300 pounds, 40-60 inches high
reproduction: 1-2 kids born May-June
status: 33 herds in isolated mountain ranges
scientific name: *Oreamnos americanus*

Imagine a mountain climber inching
across the face of a cliff. Now imagine
that he has to stay up there for the rest
of his life! That should give you a pretty
good idea of what life is like for the
mountain goat.

Fortunately for this shaggy white
animal, it's got all the right tools for
living on the highest and most rugged
peaks. Its hooves have a hard outer edge
with a soft, rubbery pad in the center.
They help hold the mountain goat to
narrow rock ledges. An excellent sense
of balance, strong shoulders, and
powerful legs also help make the
mountain goat the most sure-footed
hoofed animal in North America.

Golden eagle

other names: mountain eagle, ring-tailed eagle
habitat: rugged mountains, badlands
food: small mammals, birds, dead animals
size: 8-13 pounds, 33-38 inches long, wingspan about 7 feet
reproduction: usually 2 white eggs blotched with brown, laid in March
status: species of special concern, found statewide
scientific name: *Aquila chrysaetos*

Eagles catch and kill their prey with their feet, so they're called "raptors," from the Latin word for "grasper." The foot of the golden eagle is definitely an awesome weapon. The bird can squeeze its talons together with a pressure of 1,400 pounds per square inch. It can easily pierce the skull of many mammals.

Long ago, people thought that eagles could carry off young children. Now we know that's impossible. Under the best wind conditions, golden eagles might be able to lift their own weight. But in calm air, they can't lift more than four or five pounds.

White-tailed ptarmigan

other names: snow grouse, snow quail, mountain quail
habitat: high mountains, rocky tundra
food: leaves, flowers, buds, insects, seeds
size: about 11.5 ounces, 12-13 inches long
reproduction: 3-9 buff-colored eggs dotted with brown, laid June-July
status: native to Montana, found only in or near Glacier National Park
scientific name: *Lagopus leucurus*

The ptarmigan is a master of disguise. In the summer, its mottled brown feathers blend perfectly with the barren rock of its high mountain home. In the fall, the bird sheds those feathers and grows new ones. These are pure white, so the ptarmigan is almost invisible against the winter snow.

In the high country, there are few trees or bushes for the ptarmigan to hide in. And it can fly only short distances on its stubby wings. So the ptarmigan's disappearing act is more than just a show. It's the bird's main defense against predators.

Common raven

other names: northern raven, American raven
habitat: coniferous forests, mountains, deserts
food: dead animals, eggs, birds, insects, berries,
      small mammals
size: 2.5-4 pounds, 22-27 inches long, wingspread
      about 4 feet
reproduction: 4-6 greenish eggs spotted with
      brown, laid March-June
status: common in western third of state
scientific name: *Corvus corax*

Montana's largest songbird is the raven, a graceful, acrobatic flier. It can circle like a hawk and dive like a falcon. Sometimes it somersaults crazily through the air like an out-of-control clown.

Although it's technically a songbird, the raven has a hoarse, croaking voice. But it's one of the smartest of all birds. It can mimic the sounds of other birds and animals, and it's quick to learn.

Ravens are much larger than their close relatives, the crows. They also can be identified by their shaggy throat feathers, which look almost like beards.

Clark's nutcracker

other names: camp robber, meat bird, Clark's crow
habitat: rocky areas in high mountains
food: mostly pine seeds, juniper berries, insects
size: about 5 ounces, 12-13 inches long
reproduction: 2-3 pale green eggs dotted with
      brown, laid March-May
status: common in western Montana forests
scientific name: *Nucifraga columbiana*

This noisy bird was named for William Clark, who discovered it during the Lewis and Clark expedition of 1804-1806. Like the gray jay, it's called camp robber because it will fly into campgrounds looking for food. Sometimes it will barge right into tents or cabins. It also will fearlessly beg people for snacks.

The Clark's nutcracker mostly eats pine seeds that it pries out of pine cones with its beak. Planning ahead, it may bury as many as 30,000 of these in the ground to save for winter. It carries up to 70 seeds at a time in an elastic pouch of skin under its tongue. Even if months go by and several inches of snow fall, the bird seems to remember where to look for its stash.

Streams, Lakes & Marshes

All animals need water to survive. So it's not surprising that the 8,600 miles of rivers and almost 800,000 acres of lakes in Montana attract an amazing array of wildlife. Some of them, like the animals described here, rarely venture far from the water. Many find food as well as drink here.

It's a thrilling experience to see a wary whitetail sipping from a cool, mountain stream. Or a beaver busily patching its dam with mud. Or a row of painted turtles sunning themselves on a fallen log.

So sit quietly beside the water. If you're very still and very lucky, the animals of the streams, lakes, and marshes may come to join you.

Mink

other names: none
habitat: usually found along streams and lakes, common in marshes and beaver ponds
food: small mammals, birds, eggs, frogs, fish
size: 1.5-2 pounds, 19-28 inches long
reproduction: 4-5 kits born April-May
status: common statewide, valuable fur animal
scientific name: *Mustela vison*

A close relative of the otter, the mink is at home both on land and in the water. It can climb trees to catch birds or look for eggs.

When it comes to food, the mink likes to plan ahead. It will kill more prey than it can eat at one meal. Then it will store the rest to snack on later.

Muskrats, rabbits, and small rodents are the mink's favorite foods. It fishes from streambanks because it's not a good hunter in the water.

River otter

other names: North American river otter
habitat: streams, rivers, lake borders
food: mostly fish
size: 11-33 pounds, 35-54 inches long
reproduction: 2-3 young born March-April
status: rare in western Montana, species of special concern
scientific name: *Lutra canadensis*

The otter is one of the most playful and fun-loving creatures in the animal kingdom. It will play for hours with a pebble or a small piece of wood, juggling the toy in its paws or balancing it on the end of its nose like a circus seal. The whole family may get together for a game of keep-away, hide and seek, or follow the leader.

The game for which the otter is best known is sliding. Any muddy, snowy, or icy slope will do. The animal scrambles to the top, tucks its paws against its sides, and toboggans to the bottom on its belly, back, or side. Then it races to the top to do it again!

Moose

other names: called elk in Europe
habitat: mountain meadows, river valleys, swampy
  areas in summer; willow flats, coniferous
  forests in winter
food: young trees, twigs, leaves, tender shoots of
  plants or shrubs, water plants
size: 600-1,200 pounds, 4-6 feet tall at shoulder
reproduction: 1-2 calves born May-June
status: fairly common in western and parts of
  southcentral Montana
scientific name: *Alces alces*

With its droopy snout and donkey ears, the moose has a face only a mother could love. And a mother moose does seem devoted to her little ones. If a calf grows tired while swimming, it can hang its head or front feet over its mother's neck and she'll tow it back to shore. If a calf is threatened with danger—from wolves, bears, mountain lions, or people—the cow becomes one of the most dangerous animals in North America. She attacks with snapping teeth and slashing hooves.

White-tailed deer

other names: whitetail, Virginia deer
habitat: river and creek valleys, dense plants at
  higher elevations; sometimes open, brushy
  hillsides in winter
food: leaves, twigs, fruits, berries
size: 160-275 pounds, 3-4 feet tall at shoulder
reproduction: 1-2 spotted fawns born in June
status: common and expanding its habitat in
  Montana; secretive habits allow it to live near
  people and eat agricultural crops
scientific name: *Odocoileus virginianus*

When this deer hoists the white flag, it's not giving up. It's warning its friends to run for their lives!
The easiest way to tell a whitetail from a mule deer is to get a look at its back end. The whitetail's feathery tail is—you guessed it—white on the underside. When the deer runs from danger, it holds its tail high in the air. Often, the flash of this "white flag" disappearing into the brush is all you'll ever see of the animal.
A whitetail that wants to sneak away from danger will clamp its tail against its rump so the white won't show.

Beaver

other names: North American beaver
habitat: anywhere there's water and plenty of trees and shrubs
food: mostly leaves, twigs, bark of trees; other green and woody plants
size: 30-60 pounds, 34-40 inches long
reproduction: 3-5 kits born May-June
status: common statewide, valuable fur animal
scientific name: *Castor canadensis*

If you get "cabin fever" during the winter, be glad you're not a beaver. It spends the season cooped up inside its lodge or swimming under a roof of ice. When the surface of its pond is frozen, it can't go ashore.

The beaver's lodge is a volcano-shaped heap of sticks held together with hardened mud. It's built in the middle of a pond or sticking out from the bank. The doors are all underwater, but the single, round room inside is high and dry above the level of the pond's surface. A vent in the top lets air in.

This lodge may house more than a dozen members of a beaver family—all crowded together in a room only about 4 feet across and 3 feet high. It's pitch dark and stuffy inside.

Muskrat

other names: musquash, marsh hare
habitat: marshes, edges of ponds, lakes, streams
food: mostly water plants, some shellfish
size: 2-4 pounds, 16-26 inches long
reproduction: 5-6 kits born, 2-3 litters a year
status: common statewide, one of most important fur animals in North America
scientific name: *Ondatra zibethicus*

The tough little muskrat looks a lot like a miniature beaver. Its behavior is similar, too, and they sometimes share the same pond. But the muskrat can't topple trees like a beaver. So it builds its home by piling up water plants and then plastering the mound with mud. It chews out tunnels and a living room inside. Some muskrats live in burrows they dig into streambanks or lakeshores. These, like the mounds, have tunnels that open underwater.

The muskrat has a clever way of coping with life under the ice. It builds a home away from home called a "push-up." Before its pond freezes, the animal makes another mound some distance from its main home. The walls are thick, so when the muskrat is inside, its body heat keeps the water beneath it from freezing. During its swimming trips under the ice, the animal can climb up into this push-up to eat, rest, and catch its breath.

Bald eagle

other names: sea eagle, American eagle
habitat: nests in large trees, usually within mile of large lake or river
food: mostly fish, also waterfowl, small mammals, dead animals
size: 8-14 pounds, 34-43 inches long, wingspan 6-7.5 feet
reproduction: usually 2 dull white eggs, laid March-April
status: national bird, endangered species
scientific name: *Haliaeetus leucocephalus*

Every November, a parade of cars makes its way to a spot along the Missouri River just north of Helena. There, between Canyon Ferry and Hauser dams, the passengers watch hundreds of bald eagles feast on the spawning kokanee salmon.

Of all the birds in the nation, the bald eagle seems to have impressed us the most. Is it because the bird is so fierce and powerful? Is it because it is the symbol of our freedom? Is it because the bald eagle is an endangered species?

Fortunately, efforts to save the bald eagle have been successful, and Montanans can still see these magnificent birds swooping from the sky.

Osprey

other names: fish hawk, fish eagle, American osprey
habitat: near large lakes, reservoirs, rivers
food: fish
size: 2.5-4.5 pounds, 21-24 inches long, wingspan 4.5-6 feet
reproduction: usually 3 white to pink eggs heavily spotted with brown, laid April-May
status: fairly common in western half of state near large bodies of water, species of special concern
scientific name: *Pandion haliaetus*

If it could talk, the osprey wouldn't have kind words for the bald eagle. That's because the eagle often steals fish from the osprey after the smaller bird does all the work.

When an osprey sees a fish in the water, it dives feet-first like an incoming missile and hits the water with a splash. Sometimes it disappears under the surface until only its wing tips show. Then it rises with its catch and pauses to shake the water from its feathers. It also turns the fish until its head is pointed forward. That way, it's easier to carry through the air.

If an eagle sees an osprey make a catch, it may swoop down on the osprey and force it to drop the fish. Often, the white-headed pirate will snatch the loot with its awesome talons before the fish ever hits the ground.

Streams, Lakes & Marshes (continued)

Trumpeter swan

other names: bugler, wild swan
habitat: lakes, ponds
food: mostly water plants
size: 20-38 pounds, 58.5-72 inches long, wingspan
   6-8 feet
reproduction: 4-6 cream-white eggs, laid April-July
status: once almost extinct, still rare
scientific name: *Olor buccinator*

By 1933, there were fewer than 70 trumpeter swans in the lower 48 United States—all in the neighborhood of Yellowstone National Park. For almost a century, hunters had killed these elegant birds by the thousands for their meat and feathers and for their skin, which was made into powder puffs.

Then in 1935, the U.S. government created the Red Rock Lakes National Wildlife Refuge in southwestern Montana. There, the protected trumpeters began making a comeback. Over the years, birds born at Red Rock Lakes were successfully transplanted to other states. By 1968, the trumpeter population in North America had grown to 4,000-5,000, and the species was removed from the list of threatened and endangered birds.

Montana played an important role in the rescue of a grand and graceful species. It remains one of the few states where you can see trumpeter swans.

White pelican

other names: American white pelican
habitat: lakes, marshes
food: fish
size: 10-17 pounds, 50-70 inches long, wingspan
   8-9.5 feet
reproduction: usually 1-2 dull white eggs, laid
   April-June
status: common statewide in summer on medium to
   large lakes and some rivers (especially Missouri
   River)
scientific name: *Pelecanus erythrorhynchus*

With its huge bill, kinked neck, and impressive wingspan, the pelican looks like something out of the age of dinosaurs. It *is* actually one of the most ancient birds. It's been around for 60-70 million years, and today it's one of the largest birds on earth!

The pelican's oddest feature is its pouch, which it uses like a net to scoop up fish. Then it swallows them. It never carries fish in its pouch.

Canada goose

other names: honker, black-headed goose, calling
    goose, wild goose
habitat: ponds, lakes, rivers, marshes, grainfields
food: water plants, grasses, grain, other plants
size: 2-15 pounds, 30-36 inches long
reproduction: 5-6 dull white eggs laid in March
status: common game bird along rivers and in
    wetlands across Montana
scientific name: *Branta canadensis*

You know winter's coming when Vs of
Canada geese begin passing overhead.
Their honking sounds like the constant
creaking of a rusty swing.

These geese head south every fall to
escape the bitter winter. They fly in the
shape of a V because then each bird can
see where it's going. Even more
important, the V formation helps the
geese go farther using less energy. In
fact, they can migrate as much as 70
percent farther in a V than they can
alone. Each bird saves energy by flying
in the updraft created by the wings of
the bird in front of it. The geese take
turns being the leader.

If there's a more beautiful sight than
geese heading south, it's those same
geese winging north. They're the first
birds to migrate north through Montana,
and their honking cries tell you spring is
on its way.

Mallard

other names: common mallard, common wild duck,
    green-head
habitat: lakes, marshes, swamps, parks
food: seeds, agricultural crops, snails, water insects,
    tadpoles, small fish, fish eggs
size: 2-3 pounds, 20-28 inches long, wingspread
    30-40 inches
reproduction: 8-10 pale green to white eggs, laid
    March-July
status: common game bird along rivers and in
    wetlands across Montana
scientific name: *Anas platyrhynchos*

There are 148 different kinds of ducks
in the world. But when you say the word
duck, many people think of the mallard.
That's not surprising, since there are
probably more mallards than any other
kind of waterfowl on earth. There may
be more than 9 million in North America
alone. And the mallard is the ancestor of
the domestic duck.

With its glossy green head and white
collar, the male mallard, or drake, is one
of the easiest ducks to identify. The
female, or hen, isn't as flashy. Her
feathers are mottled brown and white.

A pond full of feeding mallards looks
like a fleet of sinking battleships. As they
pick seeds off the pond bottom with
their bills, the ducks tip up their back
ends. All you can see are tail feathers,
like the sterns of ships about to
go under.

29

Sandhill crane

other names: greater sandhill crane, baldhead, upland crane, sandhill whooper
habitat: marshes, wetlands
food: roots, seeds, grain, berries, mice, small birds, snakes, lizards, frogs, crayfish, worms, insects
size: 5.5-14.5 pounds, 34-48 inches long, wingspread 6-7 feet
reproduction: usually 2 olive-colored eggs spotted with purple and brown, laid April-May
status: common in summer in central and western Montana
scientific name: *Grus canadensis*

Watching the mating dance of the sandhill crane is a little like watching popcorn cook. The birds bob, weave, and bow to each other. Then pop! One bird bounces 6-8 feet into the air and settles down again. Then another pops up and then another.

In the middle of all this popping, males and females somehow get together, mating for life.

Great blue heron

other names: blue crane, gray crane, long john
habitat: shallow waters; shores of lakes, ponds, streams, marshes
food: fish, frogs, lizards, snakes, insects, small rodents
size: 5-8 pounds, up to 4 feet tall, wingspread to 7 feet
reproduction: usually 4 pale blue or greenish eggs, laid March-May
status: common statewide
scientific name: *Ardea herodias*

A great blue heron stands motionless in shallow water. Its head is pulled back against its shoulders, like an arrow drawn back in a bow. Suddenly the arrow flies. With snakelike speed, the bird strikes the water with its long, sharp bill. When it raises its head again, it holds the fish it has speared. It slaps the unlucky creature against a rock to kill it and then swallows it whole.

The great blue heron is a patient hunter. As it stalks its prey, it sometimes takes half a minute to lift one leg and set it down again. It may freeze in mid-stalk for several minutes at a time.

Yellow-headed blackbird

other names: yellowhead, copperhead
habitat: marshes
food: insects, grain, seeds
size: 8-11 inches long
reproduction: usually 4 pale gray to pale green
    eggs speckled with brown, gray; laid
    April-June
status: common in wetlands across Montana
scientific name: *Xanthocephalus xanthocephalus*

The yellowhead is another blackbird with a logical name. It and its relative the redwing are among the most common and noticeable birds in the Montana marshes.

Both birds share an unusual way of feeding. They poke their beaks into the stems of marsh grasses because they know lots of nocturnal insects hide there during the day. Then they rip open the stems to get at the hidden bugs by forcefully opening their beaks. This feeding method is called "gaping."

Red-winged blackbird

other names: redwing, marsh blackbird, red-
    shouldered blackbird
habitat: marshes, grasslands
food: seeds, grain, insects, spiders, berries, fruit
size: 1.5-2.5 ounces, 7-9.5 inches long, wingspread
    12-14.5 inches
reproduction: usually 4 pale blue-green eggs
    streaked with brown, purple; laid March-July
status: common in cattails across Montana
scientific name: *Agelaius phoeniceus*

It's easy to see how the red-winged blackbird got its name. The male wears bright red patches on its glossy black shoulders. Like most male birds, the redwing doesn't wear these colors just for decoration. He uses them like signal flags to declare his territory and warn other birds to keep out. Redwings have been known to attack crows, ravens, magpies, and even hawks and ospreys that come too close. They may even strike at human intruders if they think their nests are threatened.

The redwing also flashes his colors when he wants to attract a potential mate—a lot like a guy showing off his new car to his date.

Belted kingfisher

other names: halcyon, lazy-bird
habitat: rivers, lakes, ponds, marshes
food: mostly small fish, tadpoles
size: 4.5-6 ounces, 11-15 inches long
reproduction: 6-7 white eggs laid April-July
status: common along rivers throughout Montana
scientific name: *Megaceryle alcyon*

Nest-building is a major construction project for a kingfisher couple. Using their long, sharp bills and tiny feet, the pair take turns digging a tunnel into the bank of a lake or river. The job may take 3 days to 3 weeks depending on what kind of soil the birds have to dig through. When they're finished, Mr. and Mrs. Kingfisher have a burrow about 3-4 inches across and anywhere from 3 to 15 feet long. The female lays her eggs in total darkness at the end of this tunnel.

Mother and father share the job of keeping the eggs warm and raising the chicks. When it's time for fishing lessons, a parent sometimes gets the idea across by dropping its stunned catch back into the water. Then it lets the chick finish the kill.

Painted turtle

other names: none
habitat: quiet waters, slow streams, marshes
food: water plants, insects, spiders, earthworms, mollusks, crayfish, fish, frogs, tadpoles
size: 4-10 inches long
reproduction: lays 2-20 eggs in 1-2 batches a year
status: common statewide
scientific name: *Chrysemys picta*

Painted turtles are devoted sun worshippers. You're likely to see them basking on rocks or fallen logs— sometimes in groups of a dozen or more. In fact, sunbathing seems to be about as important to these turtles as eating. For every hour they spend chowing down, they spend another soaking up the sun.

As you can imagine, these sun-lovers don't think much of those long Montana winters. They hiberate at the bottom of their ponds or streams until March or April.

Painted turtles are the most common and widespread of Montana turtles.

Northern leopard frog

other names: none
habitat: marshes
food: mostly insects
size: 2-5 inches long
reproduction: lays hundreds of eggs on marsh
        bottom or attaches to underwater plants,
        breeds March-June
status: common in wetlands throughout Montana
scientific name: *Rana pipiens*

Did you ever wonder how a frog can stay underwater for so long without coming up for air? Like most amphibians, frogs have lungs for breathing. But they also have another, more unusual way to get oxygen. They can take in air directly through their thin, moist skin. When they're hiberating, frogs get all the oxygen they need this way. They can also absorb water through their skin, so they never need to take a drink.

The leopard frog is the most widely distributed amphibian in North America. It's active mostly at night. With those strong hind legs, it's able to leap 13 times its own length!

Common garter snake

other names: none
habitat: fields, meadows, marshes, roadsides,
        gardens, often near water
food: frogs, toads, salamanders, earthworms
size: 18-52 inches long
reproduction: 7-85 young born live June-August
status: common near water and in wet meadows
        and marshes throughout Montana
scientific name: *Thamnophis sirtalis*

If the word cute can be used to describe a snake, then it probably best describes the slender, striped garter snake. Of the 250 kinds of snakes in North America, the garter snake is the most common and the most widely distributed. It's active during the day and can stand cold weather. It may bite when it's captured, but it can be quickly tamed.

Like all snakes, the garter snake has no ears and can't hear. Instead, it senses the presence of another animal by feeling the ground vibrations the animal makes when it moves. It sleeps with its eyes open for the very good reason—it doesn't have eyelids to close them with!

Underwater

Montana is a fish's—and fisherman's—paradise. It's a land of clean, sparkling rivers and deep, quiet lakes set among some of the most beautiful scenery in the nation. Eighty-six kinds of fish swim in these waters. They attract more than 300,000 anglers a year.

You may not see them down there, lurking in deep, dark waters. You may not have any luck getting them to nibble on your worm. But they're there—Montana's underwater animals. And as long as we take care of our waters and keep them free from pollution, those fish will still be there another day, waiting for you to cast your line.

Paddlefish

other names: spoonbill cat
habitat: large muddy rivers and reservoirs
food: plankton
size: typically about 60 inches, rarely longer than 72 inches
reproduction: lays eggs on gravel bars of large rivers in spring
status: Montana native; found in lower Missouri and Yellowstone rivers, Fort Peck Reservoir; species of special concern
scientific name: *Polyodon spathula*

If Montana held a "weird fish" contest, the paddlefish would surely win. This strange creature with the paddle-shaped snout is a living fossil whose ancestors date back 135 million years. No one knows exactly what the "paddle" is for. Scientists think it may be a sensory organ for locating food.

Each spring, many paddlefish migrate upstream from Fort Peck Reservoir and up the Missouri and Yellowstone rivers from North Dakota to spawn, or lay eggs. Some people like to eat these eggs as caviar.

Kokanee

other names: kokanee salmon, sockeye salmon
habitat: clear, cold lakes and reservoirs
food: plankton
size: typically about 12 inches, rarely longer than 18 inches
reproduction: usually lays eggs in gravel on stream bottoms in fall
status: introduced into state in 1914; common in northwestern Montana and scattered reservoirs
scientific name: *Oncorhynchus nerka*

Next time your parents complain about how tough they've had it since you came along, tell them they should be glad they're not kokanees. Like most adult salmon, kokanee parents die after spawning.

But first these dedicated fish have to leave their lake homes and struggle upstream to the place they plan to lay their eggs. And they must undergo a dramatic change in their appearance—and not exactly for the better. The silvery male turns red and develops an ugly hooked jaw and large teeth. The female changes from gray with a dark green back to a dull red with dark red on her back.

Even in death, though, the kokanees are useful. They make great meals for bald eagles, grizzly bears, and other animals. And their decaying bodies add nutrients to the water for their small fry to use.

Cutthroat trout

other names: blackspotted trout
habitat: cool, clear mountain streams and lakes
food: insects, smaller fish
size: typically about 10 inches, rarely longer than 18 inches
reproduction: lays eggs in gravel on stream bottoms in spring
status: official state fish, Montana native, species of special concern
scientific name: *Oncorhynchus clarki*

The cutthroat was the first trout to reach the Montana area, probably about 70,000 years ago, before the last ice age. It swam here from the Pacific Ocean by way of the Columbia River and its tributaries.

Lewis and Clark first saw the cutthroat at the Great Falls of the Missouri River in 1805. But it wasn't until 1884 that the fish got its common name. A man fishing at Rosebud Creek in southcentral Montana caught some fish that he described later as having bright red slashes across their lower jaws. "For lack of a better description we called them cut-throat trout," he said.

There are two subspecies of cutthroat. They were named for the parts of the state where they could originally be found. The westslope cutthroat swam in rivers west of the Continental Divide, while the Yellowstone cutthroat lived in the Yellowstone River and its tributaries. Pure members of both subspecies have become rare.

Rainbow trout

other names: silver
habitat: cool, clear streams, lakes, ponds, and reservoirs
food: insects, plankton, smaller fish
size: about 12 inches, rarely longer than 24 inches
reproduction: lays eggs in gravel on stream bottoms in early spring
status: brought to Montana in 1889 and introduced throughout state
scientific name: *Oncorhynchus mykiss*

In Montana, no fish ends its days in an angler's creel more often than the rainbow trout. That's partly because the state has planted hundreds of millions of hatchery-raised rainbows in Montana waters in the past century.

This fish got its name from the shimmering band of color that runs along its sides. Rainbow trout that live in rivers tend to be more colorful than those that live in lakes.

Have you ever wondered why some fish have pink flesh and others have white? The answer lies in their diet. The color depends on the amount of protein and fat a fish eats. Fish that eat crustaceans, such as crayfish and water fleas, are pink. Those that eat insects and other foods tend to be white.

If you haven't had much luck with your pole and bait, you can always go see some whopper rainbows at the Arlee Hatchery or the Giant Springs Trout Hatchery in Great Falls.

Brown trout

other names: German brown trout, Loch Leven trout
habitat: lower reaches of large streams, reservoirs and lakes
food: insects, smaller fish, crayfish
size: typically about 13 inches, rarely longer than 24 inches
reproduction: lays eggs in gravel on stream bottoms in fall
status: brought to U.S. from Germany and Scotland in 1880s, planted in Montana's Madison River in 1889, common in western two-thirds of state
scientific name: *Salmo trutta*

The brown trout is more cautious than the brook or rainbow trout. Chances are, it'll be more suspicious of that lure you toss it—and so it'll be harder to catch. Maybe that's why so many fishermen go after the brown trout. It gives them a real challenge.

If you do manage to hook a brown, you can tell it from other trout by its tail, which has few or no spots. On its upper body, it has black spots and often reddish spots with light-colored circles around them.

Brown trout tend to stay closer to the bottom of streams and lakes than other trout. They're also willing to live in a little warmer water, so they can be found in valley streams as well as mountain streams.

other names: Montana grayling
habitat: historically a stream fish, now found mostly in mountain lakes where it's been planted
food: insects
size: typically about 10 inches, rarely longer than 18 inches
reproduction: lays eggs in gravel on stream bottoms in spring
status: Montana native, rare except in Alaska and Canada, species of special concern
scientific name: *Thymallus arcticus*

A bishop living in the fourth century once described the grayling as the "flower of fishes." He was probably thinking of the large, colorful dorsal fin on this fish's back.

Montana has the only native population of grayling in the lower 48 states. Most of them live in the Big Hole River and a few of its tributaries and possibly Ennis Lake. Hatchery fish have been planted in 30 or more lakes across the western half of the state.

One of the reasons the native grayling has become so rare may be its gullibility. If you catch one and release it back into the water, it's likely to take your hook again. It just doesn't seem to learn from experience. A bigger reason is that it doesn't seem to do well in water dirtied by farming, logging, road-building, and other human activities.

Yellow perch

other names: perch
habitat: mostly warm to cool, clear lakes with some water plants
food: plankton, insects, crayfish, smaller fish
size: typically about 8 inches, rarely longer than 12 inches
reproduction: lays eggs on plants and gravel bars along lakeshores in early spring
status: introduced into Montana, common in lakes and reservoirs east and west of Continental Divide
scientific name: *Perca flavescens*

Yellow perch are considered one of the best fish in the state to eat—maybe because they don't taste "fishy." They tend to travel in large groups, or schools, so if you catch one you should be able to catch more. That helps make up for the fact that they're relatively small compared to other game fish. They're also no fun to clean because they have sharp spines.

One way to identify the perch is by the two dorsal fins on its back. Trout have only one. Another way is by its color. Its sides are yellow to yellow-green with six to eight dark bands that look a little like the bars on a jailhouse window.

Largemouth bass

other names: largemouth black bass
habitat: warm, clear lakes and streams with muddy or sandy bottoms; stream backwaters with lots of water plants
food: mostly smaller fish
size: typically about 11 inches, rarely longer than 18 inches
reproduction: lays eggs in late spring in hollows it scoops along lakeshore
status: introduced into Montana, common east and west of Continental Divide
scientific name: *Micropterus salmoides*

Yes, it really does have a big mouth—the better to eat fish with. It will also swallow almost any other swimming animal smaller than it is, including frogs and baby ducks!

The largemouth bass may be the most widely introduced fish in North America. It can be found all across the continent. In the southeastern United States, where it's a native, this fish will live in water as warm as 90 degrees Fahrenheit. That's warmer than most swimming pools!

Unlike the other fish in this book, the largemouth bass guards its eggs until they hatch. The other fish in this section just lay them and leave them.

Towns, Farms & Ranches

In the past two centuries, people have moved into almost every corner of Montana. In the process, they've made life hard for some wild animals. Elk watch fences go up around the grass that once was theirs. Trout gasp for air in dirty and polluted waters. And eagles exposed to pesticides lay eggs too fragile to protect the chicks inside.

But some animals have adapted to their two-legged neighbors and thrive in their company. Maybe you thought you had to hike miles into the mountains to get a glimpse of wild animals. Little did you know they may be living in your own backyard!

Raccoon

other names: ringtail, coon
habitat: wooded areas near streams or lakes, farms, suburbs, cities
food: fish, crayfish, small mammals, birds, eggs, reptiles, insects, dead animals, vegetables, grains, nuts, fruits, garbage
size: 12-35 pounds, 26-40 inches long with tail
reproduction: 2-4 cubs born April-May
status: common statewide, fur animal
scientific name: *Procyon lotor*

Do they or don't they? For a long time, people thought raccoons washed their food before eating it. The scientific name *lotor* means "the washer" in Latin. Now wildlife experts aren't really sure. Maybe the raccoon is just finding food in the water. Or maybe water improves the raccoon's sense of touch.

Whatever the answer, there's no doubt the raccoon is a very smart and curious animal. It can learn to open tricky latches and get lids off garbage cans. As a result, some people think it's a pest—although a cute and charming one.

Red fox

other names: none
habitat: prefers mixture of forest and open country near water; also lives in suburbs, near farms and ranches
food: rabbits, rodents, birds, eggs, frogs, snakes, worms, insects, fruit, garbage
size: 8-15 pounds, 39-43 inches long with tail, 14-16 inches tall at shoulder
reproduction: 4-8 kits born in March
status: common statewide, fur animal
scientific name: *Vulpes vulpes*

For centuries, the fox has had a reputation as a sly and adaptable animal. It's certainly a clever hunter. One trick is called "charming." For no apparent reason, the fox jumps up and down, turns somersaults, chases its tail, and otherwise acts like a fool. All the while, it gradually moves closer to a bunch of birds or rabbits. These are so busy watching they forget to stay on guard. When the fox gets close enough, it suddenly grabs a member of its audience and loses all its "charm."

Striped skunk

other names: polecat
habitat: almost anywhere, especially farmland
food: insects, rats, mice, chipmunks, dead animals,
    eggs, fruits, berries
size: 6-14 pounds, 20-28 inches long with tail
reproduction: 5-6 kittens born May-June
status: common statewide
scientific name: *Mephitis mephitis*

For an animal about the size of a house cat, the skunk sure is cocky. It goes wherever it wants whenever it wants—and we all know why! After one stinky encounter, most animals stay away!

If a predator—or the family dog—is foolish enough to bother it, the skunk will try to scare it away first by stamping its feet, waving its tail, and hissing. If that doesn't work, it twists itself into the shape of a U and aims both its front and back ends in the enemy's direction. It lifts its bushy tail high over its back.

If the attacker still doesn't get the message, the skunk squirts its sickening spray at the poor creature's face. The spray is produced by two glands under the skunk's tail. It may burn in a victim's eyes, but it doesn't cause any permanent damage. Some skunks can spray as far as 10 feet. So keep your distance!

Columbian ground squirrel

other names: gopher
habitat: mountainous areas
food: leaves, bulbs, seeds, berries
size: up to 2 pounds, 12.5-16 inches long with tail
reproduction: 6-12 young born March-April
status: common in northwestern Montana
scientific name: *Citellus columbianus*

During the early summer, you can see lots of Columbian ground squirrels near the Logan Pass Visitor Center in Glacier National Park. Often mistakenly called gophers, these bright-eyed little animals live in sprawling colonies. They have sentries to watch for danger. When the shrill alarm whistle sounds, each squirrel scurries into its own underground den.

Columbian ground squirrels only leave their dens when the weather is just right. They don't like rain or extreme heat or cold. During the winter, they hibernate in chambers about 9 inches wide and 5 feet underground. Each squirrel seals up the entrance to its chamber, curls into a ball, and drops into a deep sleep. If the summer is especially dry and the food supply has withered, the squirrel may begin hibernating as early as August.

Little brown bat

other names: little brown myotis
habitat: caves, hollow trees, attics
food: insects
size: about .5 ounce, 3.5-4.5 inches long with tail,
    wingspan 10 inches
reproduction: usually 1 young born in June-July
status: common statewide
scientific name: *Myotis lucifugus*

Do you have bats in your belfry—or maybe your attic? If you do, count your blessings. Scientists think some bats can eat as many as 600 mosquitoes an hour! That's enough to make your summer evenings a lot more enjoyable.

Bats are the only mammals that can fly, and little brown bats are one of the most common bats in the world. You often see them hunting insects near water in the summer. Like all bats, they're active mostly at night.

Little brown bats use sound to find their prey. They make squeaking noises so high-pitched that people can't hear them. These sounds echo, or bounce, off objects and come back to the bats' ears. From these echoes, the bats can tell where something is, how big it is, and whether it's moving. The process is called "echolocation."

Deer mouse

other names: none
habitat: prairies, forests, rocky areas
food: seeds, nuts, insects
size: about 1 ounce, 4.5-9 inches long with tail
reproduction: 3-5 young, as many as 4 litters a year
status: common statewide
scientific name: *Peromyscus maniculatus*

The deer mouse may be Montana's most common mammal, and it has an amazing homing instinct. If you catch one and set it free somewhere else, it will find its way home again—even over a distance of several miles.

Deer mice don't hibernate during the winter. Instead, they often move into empty vacation cabins after the owners move out. And they're not at all shy about helping themselves to whatever food is left behind. These mice don't store food for the winter and must always find food to survive.

Great horned owl

other names: big hoot owl, eagle owl
habitat: forests, city parks, suburbs
food: rabbits, rodents, minks, weasels, skunks,
    birds, snakes, cats, bats, frogs, fish, insects
size: 18-25 inches long, wingspread about 4.5 feet
reproduction: 2-3 white eggs, laid February-March
status: fairly common statewide
scientific name: *Bubo virginianus*

Late at night you hear a deep, mysterious voice call "who, who?" If it sends shivers up your spine, think of what it must do to that poor field mouse racing across the meadow! The voice belongs to the great horned owl—one of the largest and most powerful owls in North America. And the little mouse knows very well "who" it's after!

The great horned owl is a fierce hunter designed to kill in the night. Its hearing is superb, and it can see even in the faintest light. Sometimes called "the winged tiger," it drops soundlessly from the sky and nabs its prey with hooked talons. It has even attacked people wearing fur hats. Apparently it thought the hats were something good to eat!

American kestrel

other names: sparrow hawk
habitat: edges of forests, open fields, pastures,
    highways
food: insects, mice, birds, bats, lizards, snakes,
    frogs
size: 3.5-4.5 ounces, 9-12 inches long, wingspread
    about 2 feet
reproduction: 4-5 white, cream, or pale pink eggs
    blotched with brown; laid May-June
status: fairly common statewide in summer
scientific name: *Falco sparverius*

For a bird the size of a robin, the kestrel packs a lot of punch. It's the smallest and most common North American falcon. And it's an expert hunter. Perched on a utility pole or wire, it scans the ground with hungry eyes. Suddenly it notices a tiny movement in the grass. It launches itself into the air, hovers over its prey, and then dives feet first, seizing a mouse with its sharp talons. Back to its perch it goes with its dinner clutched in its deadly grip.

The kestrel does most of its hunting in the morning or late afternoon. It's able to get moisture from its food, so it can survive when there's not much water.

Barn swallow

other names: fork-tailed swallow
habitat: open country and marshes, especially near
    buildings
food: insects
size: 1 ounce, 6-8 inches long, wingspread
    12.5-13.5 inches
reproduction: 4-5 white eggs speckled with brown,
    laid April-July
status: common statewide in summer
scientific name: *Hirundo rustica*

Watching a swallow chase its dinner is a little like watching a show-off pilot doing tricks at an air show. The bird swoops, climbs, and rolls, then skims close to the ground—all in hot pursuit of the flying insects it likes to eat. It scoops these up in its open mouth without even slowing down.

Because it finds its meals in the air, the barn swallow spends more time flying than most other birds. When it does stop to rest, it sits on a mud nest often built in a barn, under a bridge, or in some other manmade structure. The bird often lines its nest with chicken feathers and horsehair it finds nearby.

other names: chattering plover, field plover
habitat: pastures, plowed fields, riverbanks, mud flats,
    airports
food: mostly insects
size: 3 ounces, 9-11 inches long, wingspread 19-21
    inches
reproduction: usually 4 grayish eggs spotted with brown
    or black, laid April-July
status: common statewide in summer, small numbers
    occasionally stay the winter
scientific name: *Charadrius vociferus*

Huddled in its nest on the ground, the killdeer must feel like a sitting duck. Cattle and horses graze nearby. Dogs, people, and other intruders pass too close for comfort. What's a mother killdeer to do?

When your nest is just a scrape in the dirt lined with grass, pebbles, and stems, you've got to come up with some creative ways to protect your fragile eggs. The killdeer has two tricks. In the case of people and possible predators, the killdeer flaps around on the ground, pretending it has a broken wing. It hopes to draw attention to itself and away from the nest. It leads an intruder away until the nest is far behind. Then it suddenly makes an amazing recovery and flies off. In the case of horses and cows, the killdeer flies right into their faces and drives them away. Apparently, it knows they won't follow its lead.

Yellow warbler

other names: golden warbler, summer warbler, wild canary

habitat: gardens, yards, city parks, golf courses, wherever patches of trees or shrubs grow

food: mostly insects, spiders

size: .5 ounce, 4.5-5 inches long

reproduction: 4-5 pale bluish or greenish eggs spotted with brown or gray, laid April-July

status: very common statewide in summer

scientific name: *Dendroica petechia*

How would you like to come home and find a stranger has moved in? That's sort of what happens to the yellow warbler sometimes. A pair return to their nest after feeding to find that a cowbird has laid its eggs among their own. The lazy cowbird figures it's a lot easier to let some other bird raise its babies.

Because the warblers are so small, they can't just push the big cowbird eggs out of their nest. So they do one of two things. They either give up and "adopt" the cowbirds, or they build another layer of nest over the top of the eggs and start over. If they do hatch the cowbird eggs, their own chicks may starve. The bigger cowbird nestlings are able to hog most of the food the parents bring.

American goldfinch

other names: common goldfinch, wild canary

habitat: fields, woods, orchards, roadsides

food: seeds (especially thistle seeds), berries, insects

size: .5 ounce, 4-5 inches long, wingspread 9 inches

reproduction: usually 5 pale blue eggs, laid June-September

status: common statewide in summer

scientific name: *Carduelis tristis*

This colorful bird builds its nest later than many birds. It weaves a nest of plant fibers and lines it with the down of thistles and milkweed. The walls are so thick and the nest is so tight that rainwater will fill it up—and that's bad news for the little nestlings. If their parents aren't around to protect them, the babies might drown.

But often a parent is there. It spreads its wings like a black and yellow umbrella and shields the nestlings under its feathers until the rain stops.

43

Glossary

Alpine	Living or growing high in the mountains.
Amphibian	An animal that starts life in the water breathing with gills but changes into an adult that breathes with lungs and can live on land. A frog is an amphibian.
Angler	A person who goes fishing.
Badlands	Dry, barren land with large, sometimes oddly shaped rock formations.
Camouflage	An animal's disguise, its way of hiding from predators by blending into its surroundings.
Conifer	A tree with needles that stay green all year, such as a pine, spruce, or fir.
Continental Divide	The high ground running north and south through the Rocky Mountains that separates rivers flowing east from rivers flowing west.
Dorsal fin	The main fin on a fish's back.
Endangered species	A kind of animal that's in danger of becoming extinct.
Extinct	When all of a particular kind of animal have died and the species no longer exists.
Fur animal	An animal that legally may be hunted or trapped for its fur, such as a mink.
Game animal	An animal that legally may be hunted for food or sport at certain times of year, such as a deer or elk.
Habitat	The natural home of any plant or animal.
Hatchery	A place where fish eggs are hatched under controlled conditions.
Hibernate	To sleep deeply through the winter.
Invertebrate	An animal with no backbone, or spine, such as an insect.
Mammal	A warm-blooded animal that has a backbone. Most are covered with fur or have hair. Females have glands that make milk for their young. Men and mice are both mammals.
Migrate	Move from one place to another, often because of changes in the seasons.
Nocturnal	Active mostly at night.
Pesticide	A chemical used to kill pests, such as insects and rodents. Pesticides often are sprayed on agricultural crops to keep them from being ruined by pests.
Plankton	Tiny plants and animals that float in the water in great numbers.
Predator	An animal that kills and eats other animals. A mountain lion is a predator.
Prey	An animal that is hunted by other animals for food, such as a deer.
Raptor	A bird that hunts, kills, and eats other animals. A hawk is a raptor.
Reptile	A cold-blooded animal that has a backbone and breathes with lungs, such as a snake, lizard, or turtle. Most lay eggs.
Rodent	A mammal with large front teeth for gnawing or nibbling, such as a mouse, squirrel, or beaver.
Songbird	A perching bird usually having a pleasing song or call.
Spawn	Lay eggs.
Species	A group of plants or animals with many things in common. Most animals within a species can breed with each other. The second part of an animal's scientific name tells what species it belongs to.

Glossary

Species of special concern	A kind of animal that wildlife experts give special attention because it's rare, easily disturbed by people, or necessary for the survival of other animals.
Subspecies	A different form of the same animal, usually because of geographic isolation. Grizzlies and Kodiak brown bears are subspecies.
Talon	The claw of a raptor, or bird of prey.
Territory	The area of land that an animal, a mating pair, or a group of animals claims as its own. The territory is often forcibly defended against intruders.
Threatened species	A species likely to become endangered in the near future.
Timberline	The point in the mountains above which trees don't grow.
Tundra	A treeless area in the arctic regions where the soil below the surface is always frozen. Only low-growing plants such as moss and lichens can live here.
Waterfowl	A swimming bird, such as a duck or swan.
Wetland	A low, soggy area, such as a marsh or swamp.
Wildlife preserve	An established area in which wildlife is usually protected from hunting and trapping.

Acknowledgments

There's an amazing variety of wildlife in Montana, and every one of the critters living here is unique. I never could have written about the seventy-six animals in this book without the help of several people who've devoted their lives to the study and conservation of animals.

First and foremost, I'd like to thank Mike Aderhold, Region 4 supervisor for the Montana Department of Fish, Wildlife, and Parks, for his careful and constructive review of the manuscript. The breadth of his knowledge—and his willingness to share it—is remarkable. Bruce Auchly, an information officer with the department, was friendly and helpful even after the umpteenth phone call. Howard Johnson, chief of the Fish Management Bureau in the department's fisheries division, reviewed the "Underwater" section and offered several helpful suggestions. George Holton, of the Last Chance Audubon Society, enthusiastically shared his considerable knowledge of Montana birds. And Mike Madel, bear management specialist with FWP, helped with the descriptions of grizzlies and black bears.

Finally, I'd like to thank my family—Steve, Colin, and Jesse—for their love, patience, and support, and for letting me hole up in my office for most of three months. Sorry I missed so many of your basketball games, guys!

Gayle C. Shirley
January 21, 1993

Index

Looking for Montana's wildlife?

Look for these signs!

More than 100 of the best places to view wildlife in Montana are marked by special highway signs that show a set of binoculars. These areas have been carefully selected by a panel of wildlife experts to make wildlife viewing more fun and more accessible to all Montanans. This effort is part of the National Watchable Wildlife Program, a cooperative project between government agencies and conservation throughout the country.

To find out more about the Montana areas look for the full-color book, *Montana Wildlife Viewing Guide,* in bookstores or from Falcon Press in Helena (Call toll-free 1-800-582-2665). The book describes 109 of the best viewing areas and includes directions on how to get to each area. The book sells for $9.95.